Can You Relate?

Norma McLucas

My Thoughts, From my Heart, Through my Pen.

This book is dedicated to:

Everyone who is dealing with the headaches, disappointments, losses, problems, and all of the stress associated with life.

Acknowledgements:

My sincere thanks to my daughter, Dawn McLucas, and my mentor, Joy Mason, for their assistance, encouragement, and motivation.

ISBN 979-8-9875030-0-3 PBK

ISBN 979-8-9875030-1-0 EBK

LCCN 2022923857

December 2022

BluePrint Ambitions

blueprintambitions.com

Indianapolis, IN

Table of Contents

Chapter 1: I Believe

Life is God's gift to mankind. Some humans believe in miracles and things that can't be explained. While others only believe what can be explained scientifically and what they can hear, see, and touch.

Most people will agree that childbirth is miraculous and that it is controlled by a superior being or a higher power. Faith in the unknown, unseen, and the unexplained plays an essential role in all of our lives. I believe that we have all been faced with situations that spark doubts, test our faith, and cause us to question the Creator's purpose and his will. Although we may not understand the painful events in our lives, we know we have to accept them. Prayer plays a very important role in our healing process and our readjustment to life after the pain. During our lifetime we all will have painful events that we will be forced to endure. The same one who gave us life will help us to deal with the pains of that life.

We are exposed to miracles daily. Most of them we are unaware of, or we take them for granted. In my life, I have witnessed and been aware of numerous miracles. Once a long time ago, I prayed a silent prayer for God to heal my mother who was bedridden and terminally ill. I asked God to give me a sign that my mother would be received in heaven if it was not his will to heal her. The instant that I completed my prayers, my mother, who couldn't take one step without assistance, leaped to her feet. She ran the entire length of our house and calmly took a seat in her favorite chair in the living room. A short time later she had to be helped back to her bed. She passed away the next day.

I thank God for prayer, his blessings, his son, his grace, his love, my loving mother, and his presence in my life. I thank God for life.

Our Mother, Our Friend

Oh—What A Lady

By Norma McLucas

My first and most vivid memories as a child,

> Are filled with my mother's songs and her smile.

She was the only parent that we knew,

> But how deeply she loved us, and we did not have a clue.

We could not afford life's necessities,

> And we could only wish and dream about the luxuries.

She worked long and hard trying to keep a roof over our heads and food on the table,

> Cleaning rich folk's houses, until she was no longer able.

Her prayers were never ending, and her faith was undying,

> Even so, some nights I would awake to her crying.

Although God called her home in December of 1975,

> I still feel her presence, and in my heart, she is still alive.

Today we are all grown up, my siblings and me,

> And there is no room in our lives for competition or rivalry.

God has truly blessed us, and our mother's children we are thankful to be,

> We love and help one another, because in our family there are no big I's or little Me's.

- There is only one worthy to judge, and he is not human.

- Life is a precious gift from God, and it is up to us to give it meaning and purpose.

- One of life's greatest miracles that we can see, touch, and feel is life.

- The Creator gave us life, and we don't need mankind's permission to live or exist.

- An individual's worth should not be based on how much money they have, what kind of car they own, or where they reside, but rather on what and who resides in them.

- Stand, kneel, head bowed, head lifted, say it, think it, believe it, receive it…. prayer power.

- When you feel that you are drowning in a sea of negativity and you don't know how to swim, keep stroking. Trust your faith to be your lifeline.

- When you feel depressed or think your situation is hopeless, don't look down, look up.

- There is a counselor with all the answers. He is available 24/7, and his services are free, and his results are miraculous.

- Parents are not perfect. They are motivated by love to protect, support, and direct their children based on their own experiences.

- Parents love and support, educators teach and mold, and dedicated students mature, absorb the knowledge, and achieve.

- Life is not easy, but when we consider the alternative, most will agree that life is good.

Life is A Gift

By Norma McLucas

Live each day to its fullest, for tomorrow is not promised.

Share your blessings with those who are less fortunate, give from the heart and until it hurts.

Receive, acknowledge, and appreciate your blessings and never boast.

Give credit where credit is due, to our creator who is really in control.

Life is a gift, and it is up to us to give it meaning and purpose.

Chapter 2: Life Lessons

- An individual who chooses friends based on their similarities is placing limitations on the true meaning of friendship and will probably have very few true friends.

- Friendships are lost and relationships fail due largely to greed and envy.

- One wedge that separates family members, long time friends, and good associates is money.

- Friends should choose friends not because of who they are or what they have in common, but rather in spite of who they are not and regardless of their differences.

- True friends respect one another and will step out of character to support one another if warranted. They realize that without respect, everything else is irrelevant.

- There is a very thin line between extending a helping hand and giving someone a handout. How hard, how long, and how often that an individual leans on others, is the deciding factor.

- Consultants, preachers, teachers, and parents can provide and plant the seeds, but if the soil is infertile or in a state of rejection, there will be no growth. [Individuals must have open minds and be willing to listen and absorb the information in order to acquire the knowledge.]

- An individual's destiny or fate is greatly influenced by how they think, act, react, and how well they prepare themselves for the future.

- Learn from the past, live in the present, and plan and prepare for the future.

- Without a goal or purpose how can one measure their successes, learn from their failures, or correct their mistakes?

- Some people are quick to tell others what baggage they should carry and how they should think, talk, act, and react. One cannot be separated from their experiences, nor can they be molded by the experiences of others. Clones we are not.

- Change is not a happening. It is brought about through pain, suffering, and commitment.

- Individuals who choose to do nothing to change their depressing situations should suffer in silence.

- If one does not give respect, then they should not expect to receive respect.

- Don't let anyone, especially society, place limitations on what you can achieve. Dream, focus, study, prepare, and be determined to succeed. Positive thoughts promote positive results.

- When one gives from the heart, their lips are sealed.

- Each new day is another chance to make a difference and to live life to its fullest.

- Take pride in everything that you do, have pride in who you are, and show pride for your homeland.

- An occasional trip down memory lane may help us focus in the present and to better prepare for our futures.

- What some may consider realistic, others may misinterpret or perceive to be negative.

- Before you hitch your wagon to a star, you should do some research. Hopefully the star that you choose will not be a falling or shooting star.

- Role models should not be chosen because of their salaries, skills, popularity, professions, or the gifts that they possess. Their contributions to the world and the evidence of their good character and morals should influence your decision. Some of the best role models are linked to us genetically.

- Life is full of detours. Some are dangerous while others are adventurous. One should design, construct, and utilize concise road maps and proceed with caution.

- When we stare at the reflection in the mirror we should try to visualize and analyze the image within the image. We need to get in touch and stay in touch with our inner spirits.

Chapter 3: Been There/Done That

- If you feel that you can't respect the individual, you should respect the individual's right to be an individual.

- The tongue can be a valuable tool, or it can be a very destructive weapon. It can open doors through communication or it can inflict irrecoverable and unmeasurable pain and suffering on others. This occurs when the tongue is allowed to operate separately from the heart and the mind. [We should always think and feel before we speak.]

- When we know where an individual stands then they can't hurt us. It is only when they surprise us that we are caught off guard and unprepared.

- What one concludes or perceives is not necessarily the way that it is. It is merely their personal opinion.

- No one has a monopoly on truth. There are three basic truths, and they are my truth, your truth, and the truth.

- People who only see what they want to see, what they have been programmed to see, or what they have been told to look for, suffer from tunnel vision.

- In the workplace, evaluations should be based on observations by management and the quality and quantity of the task performed. Evaluations should never be based on hearsay, popularity, personality, or nationality.

- Don't let the fear of repercussions prevent you from taking a stand against injustices in the workplace. The people who have control are not in control.

- When the powers that be seem bent on breaking your spirit and trashing your self-esteem, exercise your self-control.

- I and me never equal we. [Individual focus cannot lead to team effort.]

- Trust is not a given. It is earned or it dies.

- One can justify anything after the fact.

- The difference between a job and a rewarding career is a degree and opportunity.

- When you climb the corporate ladder, look down on occasion. Remembering where you came from will help to keep you from forgetting who you are.

- In today's workforce, management seems to focus their emphasis on youth and degree, and very little credibility is attributed to experience, knowledge, or seniority.

- Corporate America's motto?...Increase the stress, do more with less for less?

- To be diverse requires differences. To achieve diversity requires respect for the differences.

- Biases exist in the mind. Prejudice lives in the heart and reveals itself through behavior.

- Prejudice is one's biased thoughts in action.

- A great deal of emphasis has been put on the phrase "created equal". I believe that equally as important today should be the phrase "treated equal".

- Diversity is not about special privileges for some or different strokes for different folks. Diversity is simply respect for all the differences.

- One person taking the right stand, at the right time, for the right reason can make a difference.

- An individual's place is anywhere that they choose to go or wherever they are qualified to be.

- It is a myth that one has to be raised or reside in the ghetto for ghetto mentality to reside in them. It is not limited to a location or by a complexion. It is a state of mind.

- At times we look but we do not see. We hear but we are not really listening. Sometimes we don't hear because we dislike who we see.

- Change starts and is controlled in the brain. How we think dictates how we act.

- Some people fear what they don't understand and they try to destroy what they can't change or fit into a mold.

- Constructive criticism deals with an individual's actions or other things that they can change. Destructive criticism is directed at the individual and things that they cannot and should not be expected to change.

- When dealing with people it helps to be flexible. One should be as friendly as they will let you be or as distant as they make you.

- Image is important but it is not everything. A smile does not always symbolize happiness. A solemn expression does not always signal anger or unhappiness.

- Do not feel discouraged when you are told or made to feel that your best is not good enough. This could be a true indicator that your ability, knowledge or skill is making someone feel uncomfortable or threatened.

- Individuals should not take the actions or moods of others personal unless they have done something to them personally.

- People should not project themselves into someone else's space or their state of mind unless they have been invited to do so.

- Expressed opinions based on hearsay are nothing more than worthless gossip.

- One should not let the opinions of others have a negative impact on their self-esteem. Glaring deeply into the mirror on occasion should reveal one's true image.

- Who we are today and who we can be tomorrow are greatly influenced by where we were and what we experienced yesterday.

- We are who we are and who we have every right to be. The products of our inheritances, influences, cultures, and experiences define you and me.

- People who think that they are always right, more times than not, are wrong and they are not being truthful with themselves.

- If and when one feels the need to point a finger, one should point it inward before pointing it outward. One should always do a self-analysis prior to attempting to analyze others.

- Everyone has an uncontrollable little inner voice in their head, but we do not have to let that little voice make our lips move.

- When the price of fitting in or being popular may cost you your individuality or your self-respect, then you are not getting a bargain. You are being robbed.

- The most difficult and an extremely important form of control is self-control.

- Uncontrolled anger can be very destructive.

- Individuals cannot and should not try to change one another. The choice to change or not to change is strictly a personal one.

- An individual self-respect and individuality should be priceless.

- The ability to be a great listener requires blind feeling.

- The effects of competition can be positive or negative. It is how we compete and what we are willing to sacrifice that makes the difference.

- The difference between friends and cliques is individuality.

- The instruments for measuring our success in life should not be money, power, or position. Our character, faith, morals, principles, and contributions to mankind should be our gauges.

Individuality

By Norma McLucas

I am who I am,

And who I have every right to be.

The product of my culture, experiences, influences, and inheritance,

Is the sum of what you see.

You may choose to accept or to reject. Oh.....but please do not judge,

For like you, I was created by the Creator. I am just me.

Chapter 4: Personally Speaking

- I'm with you when you are right, but when you are wrong you're on your own.

- In my world, right is right and wrong is wrong consistently without respect of person.

- I respect everyone and everyone's right to be who they are and to think and feel the way that they do. Some I have to respect from a distance.

- I am not who some think and say that I am and I have no desire to be who they are trying to make me. I am not perfect, but I'm here. Please deal with me fairly.

- I will never give up, trade, or sell my individuality, morals, principles, or my self-respect.

- To live, to love and to be loved is my formula for a successful and fulfilling life.

Chapter 5: Summary

Life is not easy, but it is worth living. Faith, family, and friends all play an important role in all of our lives. To live is to age. Information and good medical advice will help us to prepare ourselves, both mentally and physically, for some of the changes associated with aging.

Life has many phases, and it can be very stressful. We should never forget that when we appear to be alone physically, that spiritually we are in superior company. There is light at the end of the tunnel, and no, it is not a train.

Signs of The Times

By Norma McLucas

1. Your short-term memory gets shorter.
2. You clean your dentures instead of brushing your teeth.
3. Your arms aren't long enough to distance your reading materials from your eyes.
4. Your daily vitamin is replaced by prescription medications.
5. No matter how you part or comb your hair, you can't hide your scalp.
6. Your waistline grows as you shrink in height.
7. Every time you go to the doctor you hear, "This comes with age." And for this, you have to pay him.
8. Your optometrist tells you that you are nearsighted and farsighted. And when you ask him how often you will have to wear your glasses, he jokingly replies, "Only when you need to see."
9. When you dine out and the cashier gives you the Senior Citizens discount with no questions asked.
10. You think young, but your body will not cooperate.
11. You wake up everyday thankful that you are one day closer to retirement.